Hugging is habit forming.

The World According to

HUG

His First Book

by

Ted Menten

Delilah Books
Distributed by The Putnam Publishing Group
New York

I wish to express thanks to the following people.
Daniel Flynn, my editorial assistant and keeper of the spelling and punctuation.
Tina Marquis, my public relations assistant and keeper of law and order among the bears.
Burton Stillman and the staff of Pulsar Graphics, who set the type.
The entire staff of Delilah Communications, especially Lanning Aldrich,
Jeannie Sakol and Richard Amdur, who guided and inspired me to do this book.
To all my Teddy Bear friends around the world who love their bears.
And a very special hug to Florence Mills, who guided me along life's highway
since the first day I ventured into her domain, The Public Library.

A Delilah Book
Delilah Communications, Ltd.
118 East 25th Street
New York, N.Y. 10010

ISBN: 0-933328-96-6

Library of Congress Catalog Card Number: 83-46123

Manufactured in the U.S.A.
First printing 1984

This book is dedicated
to my father,
who filled my childhood
with wonder
and became my friend.

6

Looking Back...Again

Within a few weeks after the publication of my book, *The TeddyBear Lovers Catalog*, letters started to come in from Teddy Bear friends all over America and across the seas in England, Australia, Japan and even Saudi Arabia. It seems that Teddy Bears have made their way into the hearts of people all over the world. Soon there were thousands of letters and requests for *BearHugs*, our Teddy Bear publication that more or less makes a monthly appearance (if the bears aren't off on a picnic or attending a national Teddy Bear Rally).

Of all the comments and requests, the two that most often appeared were for HUG and "Looking Back," the introduction to my book. "Looking Back" was a reminiscence of my childhood, those happy, carefree days before I grew up and began passing myself off as an adult. Measuring in at 6′4″ tall and a sturdy 200 pounds, I am a more than slightly overgrown child. But I come by it naturally, because my dad is too.

As a junior (my father is also a Theodore John, as was his father before him), I very quickly became one of those apples that did not fall very far from the tree. Certainly my father was my first, and most lasting Superhero. He could even leap tall buildings in a single bound. Yes folks, he could jump right over them, and often did. The buildings were in the miniature towns and cities of his scale model railroad. There in the basement of our home was a giant system of train tracks that wove its way through mountain tunnels and over bridges, through cities and towns and far out into the farms and villages. And there in the control tower was my dad, pushing the buttons that made it all work. He would play with his railroad for hours. And, as a very young child who was even then displaying an interest in art, I would sit with him for hours and paint trees made of twigs and tiny pieces of sponge.

Upstairs, my mother and grandmother were busy ignoring the dull, humdrum chores of cooking and cleaning (which always seemed to get done in spite of this), while indulging in their own delights. Mother would be arranging the hundreds of tiny porcelain and china cats that she collected, and grandma would be crocheting another outfit for one of her dolls.

Then the big war happened and things got very serious. World War II was the last war that would unite and inspire all America, and we all pitched in and did our best. At school, we painted posters, collected tinfoil and newspapers and saved our chore money for Savings Stamps that would one day mature (as we would) and become U.S. Bonds, a magical term that meant Uncle Sam would pay us interest on our investment in America. It was a terrible war, the last innocent war, or at least the last one that everyone believed in. I grew up . . . as we all did.

Suddenly it was 1950, I was graduating from High School and getting ready to go out into the world. I spent one very uninteresting year at Pratt Institute studying art and design. Then I took off for Hollywood and the world of Walt Disney. I wanted to be an animator, and in those days Disney was the only game in town. Disney soon turned out to be very much like the Easter Bunny and Santa Claus had been earlier in life. As HUG would say, "Reality, cold, hard-edged reality." Well, I was never the type to have only one dream, so I went back to New York, where I became a commercial artist. And, as the saying goes, I made it. For many years I worked as a designer of packaging for everything from cosmetics to toilet tissue (that's the polite word for paper). In the 1970s I began designing toys, and as my body got older, my world and my spirit got younger. Soon my entire apartment was filled with toys and the ever-popular Teddy Bear reigned supreme.

Teddys had been my companions since birth. After all, if your name is Ted, all the really clever people know just what to give you on every occasion. Surprise... a Teddy Bear. But in fact, no one can ever have too many Teddys (that's a paid political announcement... my bears are watching).

At 52, I have returned to one of my first loves—cartooning. I drew my first comic strip in high school. Increasingly, they began to resemble one or more of my hero artists; Milton Caniff *(Terry and the Pirates)*, Al Capp *(Li'l Abner)*, Walt Kelly *(Pogo)* and Rod Ruth *(The Toodles)*. These great artists were my teachers. In later years, I would be continually amazed by the simple beauty of Charles Schulz and his wonderful *Peanuts* gang; and even the beloved Walt Disney continued to fill my mind and guide my hand from time to time.

Recently, in a series of interviews with cartoonists on the TODAY show, I discovered that most of these artists really considered themselves to be writers first and artists third—second place went to humor. Until *The TeddyBear Lovers Catalog*, I had written little more than a few lovesick poems. While my humor doesn't run along the lines of putting lampshades on my head at parties, I have been known to get a laugh now and then, but a writer or humorist, naw, not me. Shucks, I just draw a little (if Bunnée were here, she'd probably whack me with her stuffed carrot).

Actually, like all of humankind, I secretly believe that I could write the great American novel and have them laughing in the aisles at the Palace. After all, HUG says that dreams are the blueprints of reality, and I have a closet full of blueprints just waiting to be built into castles.

Comic strips are the world of Superheroes, and a few not-so-super heroes. By example, my dad showed me how to live the good life. He struggled and worked and struggled some more. He won a few and lost a few. He was successful by both his standards and the world's. Sometimes he failed. But he taught me a wonderful thing. He taught me that real Superheroes get dirty and tired and grumpy and discouraged and sometimes their capes get rumpled or they need a shave. But a hero is a hero if his heart is pure. And to me, Dad's heart was snow white. Now don't get me wrong, he's not perfect or flawless, but he is my apple tree, and I'm glad I didn't fall too far from it.

HUG is a modern Superhero. However, like my dad, he has his flaws. His heart is pure, but he's no wimp! When I created HUG, it was originally going to be a single character strip, with his unseen but often heard human companion. Like me, HUG was to be an only child who had control over his domain—more or less. Then I realized that no one is really alone in life, there's always the tax man. So, HUG was joined by a series of characters that would plague him and test his 'superness.'

HUG comes from deep inside of me, somewhere in the toy chest next to my heart. He is the better part of me, he is the better part of my father and the memory of both my mother and grandmother, and perhaps the better part of all the people that have written on my slate.

Bunnée is me too. She's the darker side of my Gemini nature, wanting answers and becoming furious when they aren't what is expected or desired. Bunnée, with her carrot, clobbers all that is unjust and unfair or just a plain nuisance. She is the rejected lover who loves in spite of everything. Her relationship with HUG goes back to the classic *Punch & Judy* puppets I played with as a child. Judy always had a paddle that she whacked Punch with. Bunnée has her carrot.

"Tech" is all that is modern and programmed that plagues my life and makes me believe that there is a beautiful woman under the hood of my car that really, really cares when she softly coos "Buckle up and have a safe trip." And Wendel... Wendel. Wendel is the me that is 'too big.' The me that never completely fits in ... into my shirts, into small cars and into all the tight, small boxes of life. And Li'l Buddy is the me that I want to hug, the child that I still am and always hope to be.

11

I don't know whether I was then a man dreaming I was a TeddyBear, or whether I am now a TeddyBear dreaming I am a man.

13

14

The person who creates a bear creates love.
The person who adopts a bear perpetuates it.

The child knows that a bear
will listen to his questions and woes;
and once these are emptied from his mind,
there is room to find answers.

18

19

My deeds are naughty,
but my heart is good.

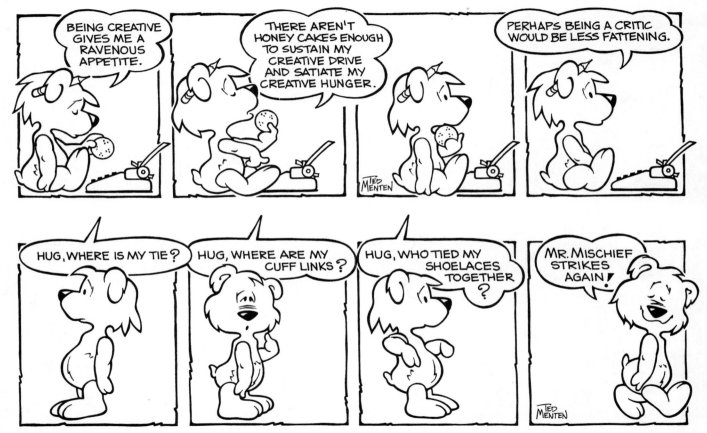

21

22

*A home without a TeddyBear
is merely a house.*

The first order of business is love,
the second is honey.

26

You cannot paint a broad stroke with a narrow brush.

Nobility is the result of being flawed and rising above it.

29

31

To live without risk is never to have lived at all.

34

*A TeddyBear does not come to life until he is loved
...but once loved he will live forever.*

*You cannot hope to succeed
if you do not dare to fail.*

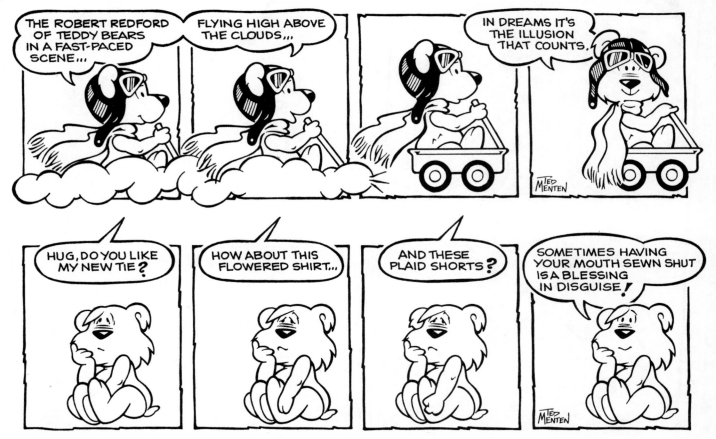

37

38

A TeddyBear may be purchased, but his love is without price.

Honey is the natural result
of a love affair between
a bee and a blossom.

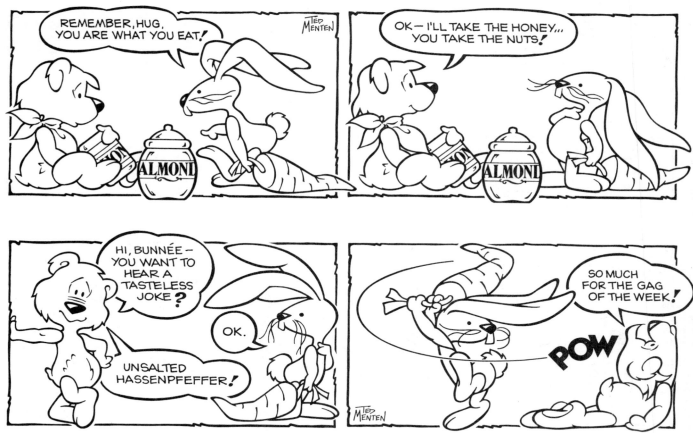

The great pleasure of a TeddyBear
is that he will not judge your foolishness,
but join in on it.

*A TeddyBear's heart beats
inside the one who loves him.*

CLICK

A KEY IN THE DOOR HERALDS THE ARRIVAL OF THE LOVED ONE.

HUG, STOP PACING

DON'T WORRY

EVERYTHING WILL BE ALL RIGHT...

YOUR FAVORITE SCARF WILL BE OUT OF THE DRYER IN A FEW MINUTES.

46

*Life's greatest tragedy
is to feel unloved.*

If you are introduced to love
when very young,
you will recognize it
all your life.

49

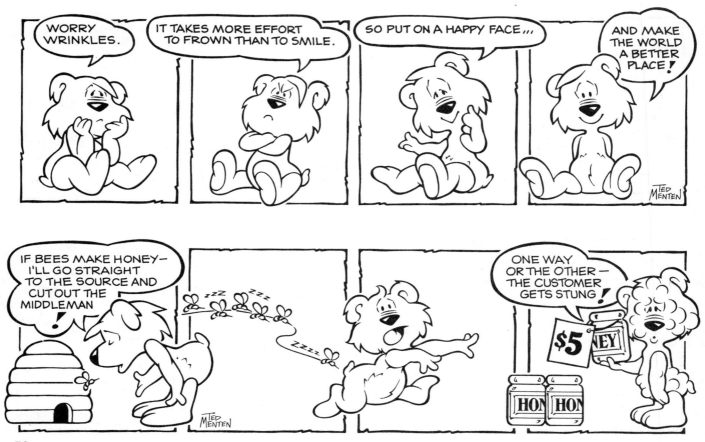

50

51

*A beautiful face
is lovely to behold,
but a beautiful heart
is spellbinding.*

53

54

I love you without reason,
but that is reason enough.

57

Kindness begets kindness. Love begets love.
Joy begets joy...this is the way of the TeddyBear.

A bore is a bear
with a loud tie and
a mouth to match.

61

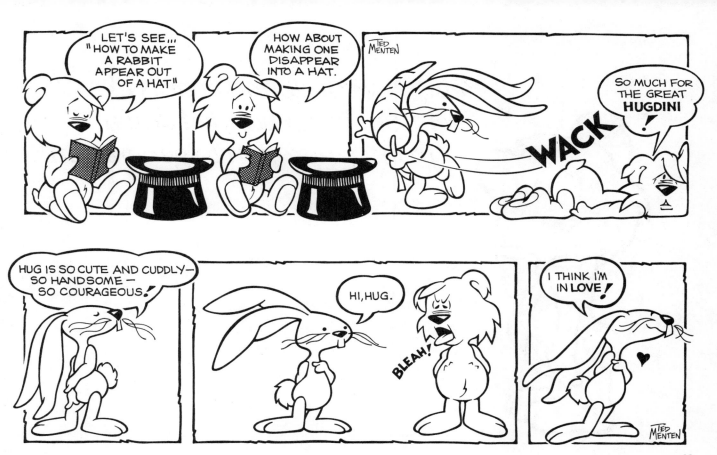

63

Being a secondhand bear is like wisdom being handed down from generation to generation.

67

*Better a sharp mind
than a sharp tongue.*

It is a TeddyBear's fate to be loved,
and his destiny to return it.

72

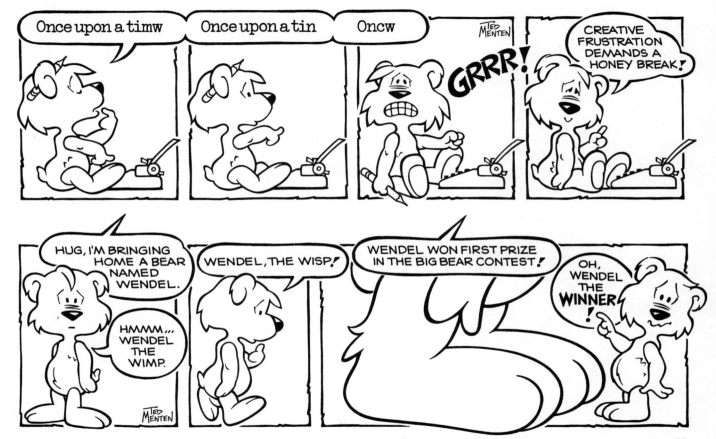

73

Hospitality is not
opening your door,
but opening your heart.

75

76

78

Bears are a dreamer's best friend.

If you do not dream,
you cannot discover what
is beyond your dreams.

HUG

BY
TED
MENTEN

83

A clown makes you laugh at him,
a genius makes you laugh at yourself.

85

*Love is a beautiful stranger
and a welcome guest.*

The proper study
of TeddyBears
...is man.

A TeddyBear
is the mirror
of a man's heart.

The HUG Club

Attention HUG fans! If you just can't get enough of HUG, here's what you need: HUG's World. It's the quarterly newsletter of HUG's beary own posh and exclusive club — The HUG Club.

HUG's World is where the saga continues with HUG and Li'l Buddy, Bunnée, Tech and Wendel. The fun never ends with games, puzzles, paper dolls, iron-on transfers and HUG's favorite honey recipes.

Members will receive advance notice and discounts on the entire range of HUG products and bearaphernalia; even before they appear in the stores!

You will be the first to learn of the developments concerning HUG's animated film debut, where and when his greeting card line will appear as well as being privy to the first of the full-sized stuffed version of HUG.

Subscribers will be the first to find out the inside scoop concerning our entire cast of characters. You can enter HUG's World four times a year for just $5.00 by writing The HUG Corporation, 300 East 40th St., Dept. HW, New York, NY 10016.

You are never too young or too old to adopt a TeddyBear and to begin a lifelong companionship of love.

BearHugs

Every issue of BearHugs is a big bundle of bear-faced pleasure. You enter a world of fun, fact and fantasy every time you open an issue.

We spotlight prominent bear makers and give away our cover bear to a lucky subscriber in a monthly sweepstakes.

BearHugs is packed with games, contests, patterns, iron-on transfers, recipes and horoscopes as well as tips on cleaning and caring for your stuffed animals.

Our appeal is to young and old alike. And of course there's HUG, America's favorite Teddy Bear comic strip.

BearHugs is the official monthly publication for International BearHugs; a worldwide club for lovers of Teddys and their critter friends.

As HUG says: "A Teddy Bear's virtue is that he cannot love himself... only others." Well, HUG's love has been returned; he has captured the hearts of Teddy Bear lovers around the world through the pages of BearHugs. Can you bear to be without a single issue?

For information write to: The HUG Corporation, 300 East 40th St., Box 28K, New York, NY 10016.

About the Author

Ted Menten is like a great big Teddy Bear. With a gentle and jovial disposition (and sometimes a big growler), he seems the perfect human to represent the Teddy Bear World.

The first printing of his book, *The TeddyBear Lovers Catalog*, sold out in just six weeks. Since then, Ted has been appearing on radio and television, including "The Morning Show" and "Hour Magazine."

Ted has authored over forty books on art and design as well as numerous articles on doll and bear collecting, and he is rarely seen without a bear tucked under his arm, whether speaking at national Teddy Bear shows and conventions or autographing his book at local book shops.

The Menten den of bears is over 2,000 strong and constantly growing. Ted and his bears live in New York City, where they enjoy a spectacular view of the Manhattan skyline and the rolling hills of New Jersey beyond.

You cannot own a TeddyBear,
you may adopt him,
live with him and love him,
and when you are gone,
he is silent witness of your love.